The Information Superhighway

Understanding the Internet of Things

Table of Contents

Chapter 1. Introduction

Welcome to our illuminating Special Report titled, "The Information Superhighway: Understanding the Internet of Things." At first glance, the topic might seem technical, but fear not! In this report, we have broken down complex concepts into digestible bites. We invite you on an adventurous journey through the vast, interconnected world of digital objects and the invisible threads that bind them. Herein, we'll break down the mystique surrounding the Internet of Things (IoT), demystifying terms like "smart devices" and "networked sensors." Undeniably, IoT is transforming our daily lives and our society, with its impact felt across homes, workplaces, and cities. By the end of this report, you'll not just comprehend IoT, but you'll be able to converse about it at your next dinner party or business meeting, as you marvel at how much technology does and will continue to shape our world. So hold onto your hats and join us as we explore the exciting Information Superhighway. Buckle up, it's going to be an enlightening ride!

Chapter 2. Introducing the Basics of Internet of Things

The Internet of Things (IoT) is essentially a network of physical objects or "things" embedded with sensors, software, and other advanced technologies. These connected devices and systems can collect, exchange, and process data, enabling them to interact with the physical world around them.

2.1. What Constitutes an "Internet of Things?"

There are several elements that constitute an IoT system: sensors, connectivity, data processing, and a user interface.

Sensors are embedded in devices to collect data about the environment or usage patterns. For instance, a smart thermostat in your home may have temperature sensors. A manufacturing facility might have sensors tracking machinery uptime or wear and tear.

Once data is collected, it needs to connect to an IoT platform or a cloud-based system. This is where the "Internet" in the Internet of Things comes into play. Devices connect via various methods including Wi-Fi, Bluetooth, Low-Power Wide-Area Networks (LPWAN), or directly through a wired connection.

Data is then processed or analyzed to provide insight or trigger action. This could be as simple as sending a routine alert ("Your front door is open") or as complex as machine learning algorithms predicting future behavior based on historical patterns.

Finally, the user interface is how we interact with the IoT system. This could be an application on a smartphone warning you about potential traffic congestion, or a dashboard on a factory floor monitoring equipment performance and alerting for potential failures.

2.2. Diving Deeper into Sensors and Connectivities

The fundamental building block of IoT, sensors, work by converting physical quantities into signals that can be read by an instrument or user. There are several types of IoT sensors including temperature sensors, pressure sensors, proximity sensors, accelerometer sensors, and many more depending on what needs to be monitored. Each type of sensor is vital to making objects "smart" and connected.

Regarding connectivity, ideal methods often depend on the specific use case. For instance, Wi-Fi offers high-bandwidth communication and is ideal for applications requiring substantial data transmission, like streaming video from a security camera. However, it's relatively high power consumption makes it less suitable for battery-operated devices.

Contrasting that, Bluetooth Low Energy (BLE) has gained popularity for battery-operated devices and short-range communication due to its low power requirements.

For long-range communication, cellular technologies such as 4G/5G are increasingly being used for IoT deployments like autonomous vehicles.

LPWAN technologies like LoRaWAN, NB-IoT, or Sigfox offer connectivity solutions for devices that send smaller amounts of data over a wider area while using minimal power. This makes them suitable for applications like smart metering, logistics tracking, and environmental monitoring.

2.3. Importance of IoT Data Processing and User Interface

Once data is collected and transmitted, making sense of it is where the true value lies. Data processing, often with the aid of artificial intelligence and machine learning, helps make informed decisions.

These techniques enable learning from patterns, predicting trends, optimizing processes, and making real-time decisions. For example, machine learning algorithms can take data from various sensors in a manufacturing setup, learn from it, and detect anomalies to predict a machine failure before it actually happens.

The user interface might seem straightforward but is equally essential to a successful IoT system. It bridges the gap between humans and these advanced technologies, allowing us to harness the power of IoT efficiently and effectively. The interface needs to be user-friendly, intuitive, and accessible to ensure the broadest possible adoption of technology.

2.4. Impact and Potential of IoT

The potential of IoT to influence various aspects of modern life is immense. From fitness trackers that provide real-time health updates to smart homes that automate day-to-day tasks, IoT is changing the way we live and work.

In the industrial sector, connected machinery and smart sensors are ushering in the era of Industry 4.0 helping businesses enhance efficiency, improve productivity, and cut costs.

In agriculture, IoT devices can monitor crop health, optimize water usage, and track livestock, dramatically increasing food production capacity while minimizing environmental impact.

With enhancements in IoT technology, network security, data analysis capabilities, and power efficiency in the future, we can expect the number of connected things to grow exponentially, intertwining digital and physical worlds to an extent previously thought unimaginable.

Undoubtedly, understanding the fundamentals of IoT isn't just about keeping up with technology trends; it's about appreciating the future trajectory of our increasingly connected world.

Chapter 3. Unveiling the Architecture of IoT

In broad terms, the IoT (Internet of Things) can be considered an intricate network of interconnected smart devices. These devices, continuously exchanging data, create a complex web of interactions executed through internet connectivity. Now, to understand this vast digital interplay, we need to dissect the architecture of the IoT and explore the components that scaffold its structure.

3.1. The Four-Tier IoT Architecture

IoT operates on an integrated, four-tier architecture: devices, the gateway (and network), the management service, and applications. Let's demystify each of these tiers.

The first layer of this architecture is made up of the 'devices' themselves. These devices could be anything from everyday items like refrigerators, thermostats, health monitoring wearables to industrial sensors and surveillance cameras. However, no matter how mundane or complex, these objects share a couple of critical characteristics: they have embedded software, and they can collect and emit data.

Table 1. Telecommunication Between Layers

Device Layer	Gateway Layer	Management Service Layer	Application Layer
Collect & Emit data	Receive, process, & transmit data	Manage, analyse, & store data	End-user application interface

A typical "smart" device comprises sensors and actuators to interact with its surroundings. Often, they possess some processing capability facilitating local (at the device level) computations, and more importantly, they have communication interfaces that allow dialogue with the broader world.

The second layer in the hierarchy is the gateway and the network. The role of this mediating component is to ensure the secure and efficient communication between devices and the management services. The gateway receives raw data from devices and can, depending on the specifics of the setting, pre-process this data before forwarding it to the third layer.

Logically proceeding, the third tier of our structure is the management services. Here, data is stored, managed, and analysed. This layer consists of servers and datacenters, which can be on-premise or cloud-based. The primary task is deciphering the data influx from numerous devices, converting this raw information into meaningful insights, and making it actionable.

Finally, at the top tier sits the application, the end-user interface, where the clarified data turns into an applicable output. Whether it is a user controlling house heating via a smartphone app or a manager analysing productivity rates on a workshop floor, this layer is exclusively about interaction with users and translating device data into comprehensive and usable information.

3.2. The Pillars of IoT: Sensors and Communication Protocols

Having established the skeleton of the IoT architecture, we must explore its vital organs: the sensors, the essential components for gathering data, and the communication protocols enabling devices to interact.

A sensor's task is to measure specific environmental characteristics such as temperature, humidity, motion, or light, and convert these into an interpretable signal. Given the huge diversity of IoT applications, a plethora of different sensors types exist. Yet, all carry the same basic principle: capturing and quantifying a physical quantity and turning it into a measurable output signal.

As remarked previously, IoT devices have communication capabilities. They can transmit sensory data and receive instructions. Different communication protocols might be used based on the application's distance, power, and reliability requirements. Some well-known IoT communication protocols include Bluetooth, Wi-Fi, ZigBee, and cellular technologies such as 5G.

3.3. Connectivity and Integration: The Glue of the IoT

Interoperability is the key enabler of an efficient IoT system. It assures seamless communication, data exchange, and collaborative functioning among various IoT components. This involves the integration of software and hardware elements that ensure unhindered communication across different IoT layers.

This integration spans three levels:

1. Network Connectivity: At the basic level, devices must be able to communicate and exchange data. This is typically achieved with a combination of local network protocols such as Bluetooth, Wi-Fi, ZigBee, and wide-area networking like cellular data or satellite communication.

2. Middleware: The middle layer is crucial for interpreting the data transmitted between the devices and the applications. It does conversions, data processing, and manages storage and retrieval. It's also tasked with ensuring secure communication and protecting data integrity.

3. Application: At the highest level, the integration happens at the

application layer. APIs and software libraries provide the tools necessary for developing applications that can communicate efficiently with all other components.

The essential thing to note is that integration isn't just about having tools and buttons; it's about creating a system of dialogue, where every component is a part of the conversation.

By now, it should be clear that IoT's architecture isn't a singular entity, but a well-coordinated orchestra of devices, gateways, management servers, and applications. It's a symphony of sensory data gathering, transmission, analysis, and response. This understanding is vital to appreciate the implications of IoT in our lives, businesses, and society at large. The next time your smartphone notifies you about a perceived anomaly in your smart home, remember, there's a highly sophisticated structure making that notification possible.

In the next part of this report, we'll dive deeper into the exciting world of IoT applications and use cases. Stay tuned!

Chapter 4. Dissecting the Key Components of IoT: Devices, Networks, and Cloud

To truly grasp how the Internet of Things operates, we must first dissect its three integral components: Devices, Networks, and Cloud. Each of these components plays a significant role in making IoT possible and efficient.

4.1. The Devices

Devices in the IoT parlance are not mere electronic gadgets. These are specifically "smart devices," designed with sophisticated software and hardware that allow communication and interaction with each other and with the wider internet. These could range from everyday objects like refrigerators, thermostats and lighting systems, to more complex devices like autonomous vehicles, drones, and industrial machinery.

IoT devices are unique owing to their embedded systems. These are compact computer systems designed to perform specific tasks with real-time computing constraints. We find these embedded systems at the heart of automation, enabling the conversion of inputs from the environment into meaningful electronic outputs. IoT devices incorporate sensors, actuators and processors to collect, analyze, and respond to data from their surroundings.

While sensors collect data (temperature, light, motion, etc.), actuators respond to this data and create an action, like switching off a bulb when not required. The processors, in comparison, are the brains of the operation. They receive, process, and deliver data, keeping the overall device "intelligent" and connected.

4.2. The Networks

Though IoT devices have the capability to collect and analyze data, their full potential would be inaccessible without a network. This is where the second component of IoT, networks, comes into play.

Networks in IoT constitute the middle part of the system, connecting devices to the internet and enabling them to communicate with each other. What really makes IoT powerful is its capacity to collate disparate data from different devices and bring them together into a unified, flexible, and instant framework of information. This network could be a local area network (LAN), wide area network (WAN), or even a personal area network (PAN) in some cases, such as Bluetooth-based systems in wearables like fitness trackers.

Different network protocols are involved in the networking of IoT devices. Some popular ones include Wi-Fi, Zigbee, Bluetooth, LoRaWAN, and 5G. Each protocol has distinctive characteristics for range, power, bandwidth, and suitability for specific use cases.

Furthermore, such networks employ Machine-to-Machine (M2M) communication, which is specially designed to allow IoT devices to exchange and synchronize data with virtually no human intervention. This M2M communication is instrumental in improving system-wide efficiency.

4.3. The Cloud

The final cog in the IoT machinery is the cloud. In most scenarios, the collected data needs more processing than the limited computing power of the IoT device can provide. This is where the cloud comes in — providing data storage, processing power, and sophisticated analysis, among other things.

Cloud computing allows devices to access and interact with complex software that would be too large or too energy-consuming to be hosted directly on these devices. It offers immense computational power, allowing for real-time data analytics—a must for IoT's dynamic scenarios.

With the cloud's centralized system, data from various devices can be processed together to produce holistic insights, often at a speed that no stand-alone device would be capable of achieving on its own. Furthermore, data stored on the cloud can be accessed remotely, enabling users and businesses to monitor and interact with their IoT devices from anywhere across the globe.

Moreover, Cloud computing empowers the implementation of edge computing due to its capacity to selectively transfer data to the cloud, making IoT a lot more effective and efficient. Edge computing allows data to be processed near the source, reducing latency and improving the reaction times of the IoT system.

The interplay between devices, networks, and the cloud gives life to the Internet of Things. Whether it is a personal IoT system within a small domestic setup or a huge manufacturing plant with hundreds of IoT sensors and devices, each setup needs these three components to function properly. As we continue to weave complex webs of connections between our devices and systems, it is apparent that the IoT, through its essential components, is ready to lead us towards a smarter future.

Chapter 5. Decoding IoT Connectivity: Protocols and Standards

The genesis of the Internet of Things (IoT) can be traced back to the dawn of the internet, but with the proliferation of smart devices, we are witnessing it take full bloom. The ability of these smart devices to interact and exchange data with each other relies on specific protocols and standards. To decode IoT connectivity, we will venture into understanding these protocols and standards.

5.1. The IoT Landscape

IoT is a network of smart devices, vehicles, home appliances, and other physical gadgets connected to the internet for data exchange. A conversation about IoT is incomplete without discussing connectivity and the role it plays. Though Wi-Fi and Bluetooth are familiar to many, in the world of IoT, a much broader range of protocols and standards are in play; some have even been specifically designed for the IoT environment.

5.2. IoT Protocols and Their Function

Protocols are essentially rules that dictate how data is transmitted and received across the IoT network. They offer a structured method for devices to communicate with each other, regardless of the type of device or its location. The choice of protocol significantly influences network performance regarding power consumption, speed, reach, and security.

1. MQTT (Message Queuing Telemetry Transport): This is a well-known messaging and data-interchange protocol designed for minimum bandwidth consumption. It's typically used for remote device communication and monitoring, and is ideal for many IoT devices owing to its minimal power consumption.

2. CoAP (Constrained Application Protocol): This is a web transfer protocol used in resource-constrained internet devices. Much like MQTT, it's designed to simplify machine-to-machine (M2M) communication, ensuring minimal overhead and parsing complexity.

3. ZigBee: This is a wireless protocol designed for home automation. It offers a high level of compatibility and can be used with various devices like lights, switches, and sensors from numerous manufacturers.

4. Bluetooth: Despite being widely used for short-range communications in wearable and mobile devices, its latest version, Bluetooth 5, boasts significant improvements that extend its range and data transfer rate.

5.3. Standards to Bind IoT Together

Just as protocols establish the method of communication, standards define its nature by ensuring compatibility between devices and systems from different creators. They are necessary to keep the expanding IoT ecosystem regulated and integrated.

1. IEEE 802.15.4: This standard specifies the characteristics of low-rate wireless personal area networks (LR-WPANs) suitable for many IoT applications.

2. 3GPP: This is a standards organization which develops protocols for mobile telephony, including 3G, 4G, and 5G, which are increasingly important with the growing number of mobile IoT devices.

3. Wi-Fi: More specifically, the IEEE 802.11 standards for wireless LANs. Wi-Fi is a popular choice in IoT environments due to its ubiquity and high-performance characteristics, mostly in settings like smart homes and offices.

5.4. Choosing the Right Protocol and Standard

The choice of protocol and standard in an IoT deployment hinges upon several factors, which can include power consumption, bandwidth, ubiquity, and the nature of the IoT application.

1. Power Consumption: Energy efficiency is crucial for IoT devices, which might be battery operated or rely on energy harvesting. Therefore, power-light protocols like MQTT and CoAP are preferred.

2. Bandwidth: Where transferring larger amounts of data is a priority, a high-bandwidth protocol such as Wi-Fi might be suitable.

3. Ubiquity: IoT applications geared towards the consumer market might benefit from using commonly known and widely adopted protocols like Bluetooth and Wi-Fi.

4. Application Nature: For industrial applications in harsh environments, robust standards and protocols like Zigbee and IEEE 802.15.4 might be required.

5.5. The Road Ahead

As the IoT landscape continues to grow, so too will the call for standards and protocols that can adapt to new needs and technologies. Technology like Low Power Wide Area Networks (LPWAN), Near Field Communication (NFC), and 5G are just beginning to make their mark on IoT.

The complexities of today's IoT connectivity are a blessing, not a barrier. A wider range of protocols and standards allows for the creation of more diverse IoT networks, enabling innovative solutions that can coexist and collaborate seamlessly. As we continue our journey along the information superhighway, it's clear that the Internet of Things and its intricate weaving of devices and data isn't going anywhere—it's steering us toward a smarter, more connected tomorrow.

Chapter 6. Understanding IoT's Role in Smart Home Applications

To dive into the role of the Internet of Things (IoT) in shaping modern home applications, we must first understand the broad concept of 'Smart Homes.' A 'smart home' can be described as a dwelling that utilizes a network of internet-connected devices to enable remote management and automation of home systems and appliances. By leveraging IoT, homeowners can foster increased convenience, efficiency, and security in their day-to-day lives.

6.1. Meet Your Smart Home

The magic of smart homes originates from the myriad of connected devices that weave an invisible web of interconnectivity. With the push of a button, or simply by the sound of your voice, you can control virtually every aspect of your home experience. Light bulbs, thermostats, televisions, security cameras, refrigerators, washing machines, and numerous other household devices can all be connected to the internet and controlled remotely. Further, through interconnected devices, it's possible to establish routines and automations, such as setting your coffee machine to brew at 7 a.m. or your thermostat adjusting the temperature based on your arrival home.

6.2. IoT: The Brain Behind the Operation

IoT is the core element that powers this intricate web of smart devices. Each device in a smart home is outfitted with sensors, software, or unique identifiers that allow them to receive, collect, and transmit data. This data can then be analyzed and acted upon, either by another device in the network or by a human user. This communication network between physical devices is what makes the Internet of Things a revolutionary concept in smart home applications.

6.3. Networking Your Smart Devices

There are a few common ways smart devices communicate with each other and the wider network to provide the convenience and automation that define a smart home. They may use a direct connection to a home Wi-Fi, a hub such as Google Home or Amazon's Alexa, or they can connect to each other using protocols like ZigBee or Z-Wave. This web of sensor-to-server connectivity allows devices to share data in real-time, enabling immediate responsivity and the possibility of automation.

6.4. Unleashing Possibilities with Automation

The ability of smart home devices to 'talk' to each other opens up endless possibilities. By leveraging IoT, smart devices can be programmed to react to certain triggers without any human involvement. For instance, your smart lights could be programmed to turn on when your smart home security system detects your presence. This sort of automation is achieved through platforms such as IFTTT (If This Then That), a free web-based service that creates chains of simple conditional statements, called applets.

6.5. The Reality of Smart Home Security

While smart home applications provide a wealth of convenience and automation, they also bring with them concerns about privacy and security. Since IoT devices are always connected to the internet, they can be a potential target for cyber threats. Therefore, strong encryption and data security practices are crucial in smart home applications. Privacy is another significant concern. As smart devices collect and transmit vast amounts of data, it's vital to consider who can access this information and how it is being used.

6.6. Embracing a Smarter Future

Despite the challenges, the proliferation of IoT in our homes signifies a transformative era. The impact of this technology is far-reaching, spanning sectors from energy conservation (through smart thermostats) to safety enhancements (via smart security systems). As technological advancements continue to improve the capacity and cost-effectiveness of IoT devices, it's certain that the smart home trend will only keep growing. The prediction for the future of smart homes is promising, as the market is expected to grow significantly over the next few years.

Indeed, the potential for IoT to revolutionize our daily living is immense. By deepening our grasp of IoT and smart home applications, we cultivate a better understanding of the interconnected world we inhabit. And seemingly, the possibilities for this new tech-enabled lifestyle are infinite.

In essence, smart homes are part of a vast interconnected world, fully integrating the physical and digital realms. It's a living testament to how far we've come in our technological journey and a tantalizing hint at where we're headed next. By understanding the expansive role of IoT in smart home applications, we have a foundation to explore further into the Information Superhighway, setting sights on an increasingly interconnected future.

Chapter 7. IoT in the Industrial Sector: Revolutionizing Manufacturing and Supply Chains

The industrial sector has always been a vanguard of innovation and productivity, leading the way with groundbreaking technologies from steam engines to assembly lines. With the advent of the Internet of Things (IoT), this evolution continues unabated. Now, manufacturers and distributors have a host of new tools and methodologies at their disposal, promising unprecedented efficiencies, increased oversight, and enhanced decision-making capabilities. This chapter takes a deep dive into the application of IoT within the industrial sector, particularly in the realm of manufacturing and supply chains.

7.1. How IoT is Revolutionizing Manufacturing

The transformation of manufacturing through IoT, often referred to as the fourth industrial revolution or Industry 4.0, fundamentally reimagines how factories function. Here, IoT combines with advancements like artificial intelligence (AI) and robotics to create super-efficient manufacturing systems characterized by increased automation and decreased human error.

Arguably, one of the most significant contributions of IoT in this context lies in enabling predictive maintenance of manufacturing equipment. Predictive maintenance uses networked sensors to collect real-time data from machinery. The data is then fed into an AI algorithm, which predicts when the equipment might malfunction or require maintenance. This astounding innovation, a clear departure from the traditional reactive approach, dramatically cuts down on the need for routine check-ups, you can imagine the cost savings this can potentially generate!

Beyond maintenance, IoT also has implications for production line efficiency. 'Smart' manufacturing equipment can identify bottlenecks or inefficiencies in the production line in real-time, recommend solutions, and even implement fixes autonomously. This not only reduces production downtime but also increases product quality.

Moreover, IoT enables manufacturers to create 'digital twins' - detailed virtual replicas of physical systems. By simulating how a product or process performs under various conditions, these models help identify issues before they occur in the physical world, reducing setbacks and increasing efficiency.

What's more, the advent of IoT has made remote operations more feasible than ever before. This capability allows central oversight of multiple increase in off-site manufacturing facilities, reducing travel costs, and enabling rapid response to issues.

7.2. IoT in Supply Chain: Maximizing Efficiency and Transparency

Just as in manufacturing, IoT has the potential to revolutionise supply chain operations as well. A compelling manifestation of this can be seen in inventory management.

Smart warehouses enabled by IoT technology can automate inventory management, increasing accuracy while decreasing the need for manual labor. IoT sensors can track inventory levels in real-time, automating reordering processes and reducing the risk of overstocking or understocking.

One tremendous advantage of IoT in the supply chain landscape is the facilitation of real-time tracking of goods in transit. IoT-enabled RFID and GPS systems help companies keep track of shipments in real-time, giving them tighter control over delivery times and minimizing uncertainty in their logistics.

Furthermore, IoT can also add a level of intelligence to the way we handle product lifecycle management. IoT devices in the 'smart packaging' realm can monitor product conditions during transit, ensuring that items arrive at their destination in optimal conditions. This is particularly valuable in the pharmaceutical and food and beverage industries, where maintaining the right temperature or humidity levels can be vital.

7.3. IoT and Cyber Physical Systems: The Future of Industrial Sector

Finally, it is essential to discuss Cyber-Physical Systems - the advanced stage of IoT application in the industrial sector. CPS refers to a system of collaborating computational elements controlling physical entities. By merging physical systems with software and network control, cyber-physical systems go a step beyond traditional IoT networks, enabling higher levels of autonomy, resiliency, and performance. They introduce exciting opportunities in fields such as autonomous vehicles, smart grids, and industrial automation.

In conclusion, the potential applications of IoT in the industrial sector are vast and transformative. These technologies promise to add fresh layers of efficiency, intelligence, and control over our manufacturing and supply chain processes, making the industrial sector a fascinating frontier in the IoT revolution. There are, of course, challenges to be overcome, including data security and privacy concerns, and integration issues with legacy systems. But with the massive potential benefits on offer, the momentum behind industrial IoT is unlikely to stall.

The revolution is here, and it is digitized, interconnected, and intelligent. As the Internet of Things continues to penetrate deeper into our industrial systems, it promises to redefine productivity as we know it, sculpting a future where our industries are smarter, more efficient, and more sustainable than ever before.

Chapter 8. Healthcare and IoT: A Digital Healing Touch

The world of healthcare is not impervious to the transformative powers of technology. With the growing prevalence of the Internet of Things, infusing healthcare with a digital healing touch is no longer a lofty ambition but a vibrant reality.

8.1. The Promise of IoT in Healthcare

The healthcare sector offers a myriad of opportunities for IoT integration. Facilities adopt these smart technologies worldwide to improve patient care, efficiency, and the overall experience. IoT, simply put, is a network of devices exchanging and analyzing data without human intervention. In healthcare, this data comes from various sources: wearable fitness trackers, implanted devices, and built-in sensors in medical equipment, to name a few.

Assume a heart failure patient with an IoT-enabled pacemaker, for example. This device continuously monitors the patient's heart rate and rhythm, automatically alerting the healthcare provider if there is a substantial deviation from normal patterns. This immediate notification can potentially save lives, speaking volumes about IoT's impact on patient care and outcomes.

8.2. Characteristics of Healthcare IoT Devices

Devices incorporated in healthcare IoT ecosystems often share several advantageous features:

- Remote Monitoring: These devices enable real-time tracking of a patient's vital signs, facilitating necessary intervention when parameters stray from the normal range.

- Data Accumulation: IoT devices collect considerable data over time, generating comprehensive patient profiles that aid in diagnosis and treatment planning.

- Preventive Care: With continuous monitoring, healthcare providers can predict possible health issues, allowing for preventive measures instead of reactive treatment.

- Enhanced Patient Experience: By providing personalized care, improved monitoring, and reduced hospital stays, IoT enhances overall patient experience and satisfaction.

- Cost-effectiveness: IoT reduces hospital readmissions and unnecessary visits, resulting in substantial cost savings for both patients and healthcare facilities.

8.3. Common Healthcare IoT Applications

There are numerous applications of IoT within the healthcare sector, here are some examples:

- Wearable devices: These include fitness bands, smartwatches, and more sophisticated devices like insulin pumps or heart monitors. They record and share health data in real-time, leading to more precise treatments.

- Remote Patient Monitoring: These systems allow the healthcare team to monitor patients outside conventional clinical settings, enhancing access to care and reducing healthcare delivery costs.

- Smart Hospitals: Sensors and wearable devices collect patient data, which is then analyzed by Artificial Intelligence (AI) to optimize treatments and improve patient care.

- Asset Tracking: IoT sensors help in tracking medical equipment, personnel, and patients within the healthcare facility, increasing efficiency and patient safety.

8.4. The Challenges in Implementing IoT in Healthcare

Although there are significant potential benefits, healthcare institutions face a range of challenges when implementing IoT.

- Privacy and Security: The handling of sensitive personal and health information presents a significant risk. Hackers targeting IoT devices can lead to data breaches, with severe implications for patient privacy and safety.

- Interoperability: Devices from various manufacturers may not be compatible, impeding the smooth operation of an interconnected system.

- Infrastructure Requirements: Healthcare facilities require robust network facilities and secure cloud storage to support IoT systems.

8.5. The Future of IoT in Healthcare

Despite these challenges, the future of IoT in healthcare is promising. A significant part of the IoT's future in healthcare involves using Big Data and AI, whereby medical data collected by IoT devices will be analyzed to provide insights into health trends, predictive analysis for various diseases, and more.

IoT could also extend the reach of healthcare services to remote locations. Remote patient monitoring could bring quality healthcare to rural areas where accessing a healthcare facility poses a challenge.

The healthcare landscape has been forever changed by the Internet of Things, and while we are only at the cusp of this technological revolution, the possibilities it promises are truly transformative.

Chapter 9. Smart Cities: How IoT is Redefining Urban Spaces

As we continue our exploration of the Internet of Things (IoT), imagine stepping into a city where public transportation runs flawlessly, energy is conserved, traffic congestion is a thing of the past, and the quality of life is elevated. These are not science fiction shadows, but potential realities of a Smart City fueled by IoT technology.

IoT's role in shaping smart cities hinges on seamless connectivity and the application of data collected from numerous devices or "things" to bring about a beneficial transformation in our urban spaces. The vision is to realize a city where technology and data are utilized to enhance inhabitants' quality of life, efficiently use resources, and reduce environmental footprint. This detailed and exhaustive exploration will take you through various components of Smart Cities from IoT's perspective and it's transformative power in redefining urban spaces.

9.1. The Building Blocks of Smart Cities

To understand the magnanimity of smart cities, it's crucial to unpack the primary components that are driven by IoT.

First, smart grids play a key role in enhancing energy efficiency. These grids use information about the behaviors of electricity suppliers and consumers in an automated fashion to improve the efficiency, reliability, and sustainability of electricity distribution.

Next, we have smart water solutions, which monitor and maximize the efficiency of water use, either through smart irrigation systems or by identifying and rectifying water leakage issues in the city's infrastructure.

Smart home technology is another pillar, offering homeowners comfort, energy efficiency, and security through connected devices that can be controlled remotely through smartphone apps or AI-powered virtual assistants.

Lastly, IoT devices contribute to smart transportation systems, reducing road congestion, improving air quality, and enhancing citizens' safety through intelligent traffic management systems and autonomous rapid transit systems.

9.2. Harnessing the Power of Data

The core premise of a smart city is the manipulation of information to optimize resources, and this is fundamentally driven by data. Different IoT devices, sensors and advanced technologies, such as AI, capture, transmit, and analyze this data to bring about actionable insights.

For instance, sensors on public trash cans can emit a signal when they're nearing capacity, alerting waste management services about the best time for pickup. Additionally, IoT sensors can monitor noise, air purity, or radiation levels, effectively detecting hazardous conditions and enabling faster responses.

Data also plays a crucial role in predictive analytics, whereby collected information can be analyzed to predict future trends. Take traffic management as an example. Data collected from traffic sensors can be analyzed to predict congestion times, and city councils can use this information to manipulate traffic light timings or suggest alternative routes to commuters, thus reducing congestion and saving time.

9.3. The Pillars of Connectivity

An efficient network infrastructure is a fundamental requirement for smart cities. Some of the key technologies enabling IoT communication in smart cities include:

- 5G and Beyond: These technologies are touted as game-changers for the future connectivity requirements of smart cities, capable of handling high-speed, real-time data transmission with minimal latency.

- Wi-Fi 6: An upgrade of the traditional Wi-Fi, which can service more devices at higher speeds and includes better service quality.

- Low Power Wide Area Networks (LPWANs): These include networks like Narrowband IoT (NB-IoT) and LTE for Machines (LTE-M), which cater to the needs of a vast number of low-power devices and sensors prevalent in a smart city's ecosystem.

- Satellite Internet: Offers a solution for areas where traditional forms of connectivity are difficult to establish.

9.4. The Path to Urban Sustainability

In smart cities, sustainability dovetails with efficiency. IoT applications in a smart city can lead to significant energy savings, reduce CO_2 emissions, and optimize waste management.

Energy-saving starts with smart buildings and homes that automatically adjust heating and lighting based on occupancy or time of the day. Smart grids can balance power loads during peak times, reducing stress on power plants and reducing the need for additional energy-generating facilities.

On the other hand, sensor-enabled waste management systems allow pickups based on real-time need rather than pre-fixed schedules, saving fuel and workforce, and enabling efficient waste management. Similarly, smart transportation systems aim for a considerable reduction in traffic congestion, fuel consumption, and the resulting emissions.

9.5. Security and Privacy: The Twin Challenges

Despite the broad potential of smart cities, they are not immune to challenges. The debate around security and privacy is primary, as the increase in connected devices presents more potential gateways for cybercriminals.

Privacy is another concern. The vast amounts of data collected by various devices, if not properly secured, could lead to sensitive information getting into the wrong hands. Policies and regulatory guidelines need to be put in place to ensure that privacy and ethical concerns are addressed without compromising the utility of collected data.

9.6. The Future of Smart Cities

While IoT is the underpinning of today's smart cities, the future will likely see the entrenchment of advanced machine learning algorithms and AI. As more cities chart the journey towards becoming 'Smart', the amalgamation of human intelligence, AI, and data will re-define urban spaces.

From improving everyday conveniences and combatting climate change to creating safer public spaces and systems, IoT's role in shaping Smart Cities is indefinite. By understanding, we can be a conscious participant in this future, deciding how we will live, work, and play in the cities of tomorrow.

Chapter 10. Security and Privacy Concerns in IoT

As the pervasiveness of the IoT expands, so, unfortunately, does the potential for security and privacy vulnerabilities. These concerns are multi-layered, encompassing everything from individual device security to the robustness of the overall network. Let's delve into this critical aspect to understand its magnitude and importance.

With grander connectivity comes greater risk; a universal principle that has scant regard for technological advancements. In the context of the IoT, this escalated risk touches on both personal privacy and public safety. The trade-off between unprecedented convenience and potential exposure is a delicate one, requiring a thoughtful and meticulous approach.

10.1. The Breach-avenue: IoT Device Security

Any discourse on IoT security must commence with the devices themselves. Despite seeming innocuous, they represent the easiest point of entry for malicious entities. This gateway into the network is due largely to the often limited cybersecurity measures on these devices. Many IoT devices have weaker authentication methods, while others are not consistently updated, leaving them vulnerable to exploits.

These vulnerabilities can be categorized broadly into device vulnerabilities and network vulnerabilities. Device vulnerabilities pertain mostly to software bugs and hardware flaws. For instance, a camera with weak password protection could be easily accessed. Network vulnerabilities, on the other hand, relate to poorly secured communication channels between IoT devices, which can be intercepted by malicious entities.

10.2. The Erosion of Personal Privacy

Beyond the danger posed to the device and its network is the potential erosion of personal privacy. With IoT devices' daily utilization ranging from health monitoring devices to smart home applications, vast amounts of personal data are constantly collected, processed, and transmitted. While this data equips IoT devices with the ability to offer personalized services and convenience, it can also be used to assemble a detailed profile of an individual's behavior and preferences when falling into the wrong hands.

Frighteningly, the detailed access which IoT devices provide into people's lives can arm a potential attacker with unprecedented knowledge. Imagine a smart thermostat revealing when you are away from home or a smart TV eavesdropping on your conversations. The implications of these are far-reaching, extending to identity theft, stalking, and even home break-ins.

10.3. Cybersecurity in the Era of IoT: A New Paradigm

To contend with IoT's complex security concerns, we must revisit traditional notions of cybersecurity. Previously, the focus was on securing endpoints and perimeter defenses — a strategy that becomes wholly inadequate when dealing with a multitude of connected devices that form the IoT.

Instead, security for the IoT must be comprehensive and holistic, encompassing the lifetime of each device, from the design stage to decommissioning. A robust IoT network considers first device production with secure firmware and hardware to ensure robust device security. The network configuration is important too, incorporating security features like data encryption and strong authentication protocols to protect the communication channels.

10.4. IoT Regulations and Standards

The road to IoT security is convoluted, but it is being simplified by the ongoing development of security standards and regulations. Standards bodies, such as the Institute of Electrical and Electronics Engineers (IEEE), and governments have been working towards creating comprehensive regulatory frameworks and best practice guidelines to aid in securing IoT devices.

Some of the most significant progress in this area has been the creation of regulations like the European Union's General Data Protection Regulation (GDPR), which enforces rigorous data protection protocols, including those where IoT devices are concerned.

10.5. Conclusion: The Balancing Act

Security and privacy in the age of IoT is an intricate dance. As we strive for technological advancements, we must also be unrelenting in our continuous pursuit of robust protective measures. Through a comprehensive and strategic approach to IoT security, incorporating personal device security, network protection, regulatory adherence, and an unwavering commitment to privacy, we can enjoy the many benefits IoT offers with a peace of mind. Despite the challenges, the promises this technology holds far outweigh its growing pains. Embracing this reality is paramount to successfully venturing further into the interconnected and exciting world of IoT.

Chapter 11. The Future Vision: IoT and The Road Ahead

The journey of Io has been notably energetic over the last decade. It started as a mere brushstroke of visionaries, a hint of a future unimaginable. Yet, today, it sits on the brink of mainstream adoption, already transforming our everyday lives, homes, workplaces, cities, and industries. Yet despite the progress made, the road ahead is long, winding, and not without its own challenges and opportunities.

11.1. The Dream: Society 5.0 and the IoT

Society 5.0, a term coined by Japan, represents the next stage in the evolution of societal development, following the Information Society (Society 4.0). At the heart of Society 5.0, lies the concept of hyper-connectivity, made possible by technology, and more specifically, IoT.

In Society 5.0, people, devices, systems, and companies are interconnected through IoT. Data flows seamlessly from one entity to another, leading to real-time analytics, autonomous operations, and intelligent solutions that enhance our lifestyle, efficiency, and productivity. Smart homes become more intuitive, smart cities more efficient, and industries more sustainable and productive.

Yet, the vision extends beyond just improving efficiency. It's about creating a society that collaboratively solves global issues such as climate change, demographic shifts, and economic inequality. Thanks to IoT, Society 5.0 aims to balance economic advancement with the resolution of social problems by offering a human-centered society.

11.2. The Trials: Addressing IoT Challenges

Despite the promising vision, the road to ubiquity for IoT is streaked with challenges, mainly falling into three categories: technical, security, and privacy.

Technical challenges pertain to aspects like data management and interoperability. With billions of devices interconnected, the amount of data generated would be immense. How do we collect, store, analyze, and gain insights from large-scale data in real-time? Additionally, devices and systems from different manufacturers and vendors need to speak the same language, demanding standardized data format and communication protocols.

Security risks, on the other hand, stem from the very interconnectedness that makes IoT so powerful. Each additional device added to a network represents a potential vulnerability - an entry point for unwanted intrusions.

Privacy is perhaps the most significant societal concern tied to the IoT. As devices collect, analyze, and share personal data, issues of access control and data protection will come to the forefront.

11.3. The Solutions: Crafting a Roadmap

To fully actualize the promise of IoT and mitigate its challenges, we need a roadmap that adapts as technology and society evolve. This roadmap may involve things like:

1. Setting international standards for data exchange and security protocols.

2. Innovative data management solutions integrating IoT and Big

Data technologies.

3. A legal and regulatory framework to protect privacy, where technology companies, activists, and governments collaborate.

4. Public education on IoT technologies to enhance its acceptance and smart usage.

11.4. The Reality: IoT Implementation

Implementation of IoT is already underway in various sectors. For instance, Industry 4.0 uses IoT to create smart factories. Healthcare employs wearable and implanted devices for remote monitoring. Retail leverages predictive analysis from customer data to personalize shopping experiences. These are but a few of the sectors embracing IoT, and the list will certainly continue to expand.

11.5. IoT and Tomorrow

The Internet of Things is transformative, poised to reshape our society profoundly. Its potential is virtually limitless, given the increasing ubiquity of internet connectivity and the exponential growth of smart devices.

From a user perspective, IoT is set to further enhance convenience, providing more intuitive interfaces, and allowing for even more personalized experiences. From the broader societal and industrial point of view, IoT has the potential to drive significant advancements in productivity, efficiency, and sustainability.

However, to unlock the full potential of IoT, stakeholders need to collaboratively address the many associated challenges. The fulcrum of the roadmap involves balancing the thrill of exponential possibilities with the careful and responsible management of societal and technical challenges. It is only then can we fully harvest the fruits of the Internet of Things. This, then, is our vision of the road ahead for the Internet of Things.

The information superhighway lies open, inviting us all on an adventurous journey into an interconnected future, ably led by the Internet of Things. Buckle up, lest you miss the ride of your lifetime!